The Nature Kid's Guide to

ANTS

DAVID ANDERSON

LP Media Inc. Publishing
Text copyright © 2026 by LP Media Inc.

For information address LP Media Inc. Publishing,
30012 Variolite St NW, Princeton MN 55371
www.lpmedia.org

Publication Data

Ants
The Nature Kid's Guide to Ants — First edition.

Summary: "Learn all about Ants, the Nature Kid Way"
— Provided by publisher.

ISBN: 979-8-89818-197-0

[1. Ants – Non-Fiction] I. Title.

Title: The Nature Kid's Guide to Ants

CONTENTS

AWESOME ANTS

Crunch! A tiny ant drags a seed bigger than itself.

Look out! Beneath your feet, millions of tiny workers are busy tunneling, carrying, and building. Ants are some of the hardest working creatures on Earth and they are almost everywhere you look.

Ants come in many sizes, but do not let their small bodies fool you. An ant can lift up to 50 times its own body weight. That is like you lifting a car over your head!

Ants live together in large groups called colonies. Some colonies have just a few hundred ants. Others hold millions. But no matter the size, every single ant has a job and every single ant does it.

MIGHTY MOUTHS

Ants have two stomachs — one for themselves and one just for carrying food back to share with the whole colony!

Click! An ant snaps its strong jaws shut on a leaf.

An ant has three main body parts. The head holds its eyes and mouth. The middle part is called the **thorax**, and six legs attach there. The back part is the abdomen.

Ants have two long feelers on their heads called **antennae**. These feelers are amazing tools! Ants use them to smell, touch, and taste the world around them.

Strong jaws called **mandibles** help ants bite and carry food. Some ants have jaws so powerful they can cut through tough leaves like tiny scissors.

ANT TEAMWORK

Some queen ants can live for over 30 years!

Patter! Thousands of ants move together like one giant creature.

An ant **colony** works like one big body. Each ant has a job. The queen lays eggs. Worker ants find food and build tunnels. Soldier ants guard the nest from danger.

No single ant is in charge. The colony makes choices as a group. When one worker finds food, others follow the scent trail to help carry it home.

Some people call a colony a superorganism. That means many ants act as one living thing. It is like every ant in the colony shares the same brain!

SPEAKING ANT

Sniff! An ant taps its feelers and picks up a secret trail.

Ants talk without making a sound. They use special scents called **pheromones**. An ant leaves a tiny smell trail as it walks, and other ants follow the trail to find food.

Different smells mean different things. One scent says, 'Food is this way!' Another warns, 'Danger, run!' Ants read these messages with their antennae.

This scent system works like a secret code. Millions of ants can share news in minutes. The whole colony stays connected through smell, even in the dark underground.

FIERY FIGHTERS

Fire ants survive floods by linking legs to form a living raft that floats for weeks!

Watch out! A fire ant stretches and pushes out its stinger.

Fire ants get their name from their painful sting. It burns like fire! These red and brown ants came from South America. Now they live in warm places all over the world.

Fire ants build big dirt mounds in fields and yards. A single mound can hold over 200,000 ants. Bump the mound, and hundreds rush out to attack!

These fierce ants eat bugs, seeds, and even small animals. They work together to catch prey much bigger than themselves. A team of fire ants can take down a lizard!

BULLET BLAST

In one tribe in Brazil, young people wear gloves full of stinging bullet ants to prove they are brave!

Zap! A bullet ant delivers the most painful sting on Earth.

Bullet ants live in rain forests of Central and South America. These ants are giants in the ant world! One bullet ant can be as long as your thumb tip — about one inch.

Bullet ants get their name because their sting hurts so much. Some people describe it as feeling like being shot by a bullet! The pain lasts for a whole day. Most animals learn to stay far away from these ants.

Bullet ants nest in small groups near the base of trees. They hunt at night, climbing high into the canopy to find insects to eat. Their size and sting make them fearsome hunters.

FUNGUS FARMERS

Leafcutter ants can strip all the leaves from a tree in just one night!

Snip! A leafcutter ant clips a piece of green leaf and carries it home.

Leafcutter ants do not eat leaves. They use leaves to grow food! These clever ants chew up leaf bits and pile them inside their nest. A special fungus grows on the pile, and the ants eat the fungus.

Long lines of leafcutter ants march through the forest. Each one holds a leaf piece above its head. They look like tiny green flags waving in the wind.

Leafcutter ants live in Central and South America. Their underground nests can be as big as a house, with thousands of rooms and tunnels.

MARCHING MILLIONS

Whoosh! A swarm of army ants surges across the forest floor.

Army ants never stay in one place. They march through the forest in huge columns, eating everything in their path. When they stop to rest, they grab onto each other and form a living shelter made entirely out of their own bodies!

Millions of army ants sweep across the ground like a dark churning river. Insects, spiders, and even small lizards scramble to escape.

Here is the really surprising part: army ants are almost completely blind! They follow chemical trails and navigate entirely by touch and smell. They cannot see a thing, yet they move like one giant unstoppable machine.

CARPENTER CREWS

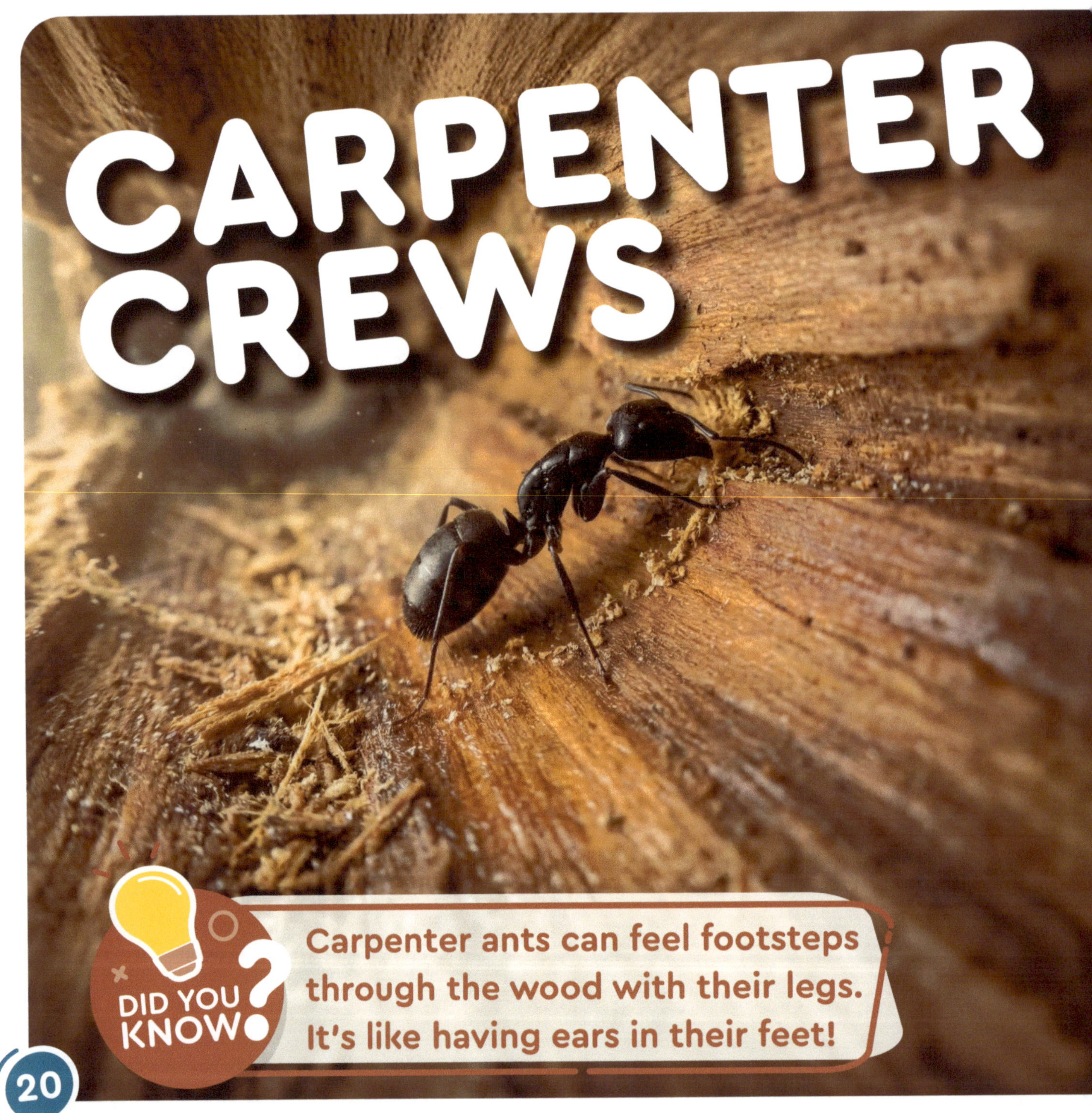

Scrape! A carpenter ant chews a tunnel deep inside a log.

Carpenter ants are big, black ants that love wood. But they do not eat it! They chew tunnels through damp wood to make their nests. Tiny sawdust piles show where they have been digging.

These ants can live in dead trees, old stumps, and even wooden houses. People do not like finding them chewing inside their walls!

Carpenter ants come out at night to look for food. They eat sweet things like fruit juice and honeydew from tiny bugs called aphids. Their smooth tunnels can stretch for many feet through a single log.

HONEY POTS

People in Australia dig up honeypot ants and eat them like candy — they taste like honey!

22

Pop! A honeypot ant swells up like a shiny golden grape.

Honeypot ants have a wild trick. Some ants in the colony fill up with sweet liquid until their bellies swell like tiny balloons. These living storage tanks hang from the ceiling of the nest.

When other ants get hungry, they tap a honeypot ant on the mouth. The swollen ant spits up a drop of sweet food to share. It is like having a snack machine in your home!

Honeypot ants live in dry deserts where food is hard to find. Storing food this way helps the colony survive the long, hot months when there is nothing else to eat.

LEAF STITCHERS

Rustle! A weaver ant pulls two leaves together to build a nest.

Weaver ants build nests out of living leaves high in the trees. Adult ants pull two leaves close together. Then they gently squeeze a larva, and it makes silk thread to glue the leaves shut!

One colony can have many leaf nests spread across several trees. The ants run along branches and connect their homes with trails. Some colonies have over 100 nests!

Weaver ants live in tropical forests in Asia, Africa, and Australia. They are green or orange and are fierce fighters. These ants guard their leaf homes and will attack anything that comes near!

JAW JOLT

A trap-jaw ant can snap its jaws against the ground to launch itself backward through the air like a tiny rocket!

Snap! A trap-jaw ant slams its jaws at blazing speed.

Trap-jaw ants have the fastest jaws in nature. Their jaws snap shut at over 140 miles per hour! That is faster than most cars on the highway.

These ants use their super jaws to catch prey. A trap-jaw ant holds its mouth wide open and waits. When a bug gets close — snap! The jaws slam shut in less than one millisecond.

Trap-jaw ants live in warm forests and grasslands. They hide in leaf litter on the ground and wait for their next meal to wander by.

BLAST SACRIFICE

Scientists only gave exploding ants their official name in 2018 — they were a mystery for over 100 years!

Boom! An exploding ant bursts open to save its colony.

Some ants will do anything to protect their colony. Exploding ants from Southeast Asia have a wild way to fight. When an enemy gets too close, the ant squeezes its own body until it pops!

Sticky yellow goo sprays out from its head and traps the attacker. The ant dies, but the rest of the colony stays safe. It is a brave sacrifice that saves many lives.

These small ants live in the treetops. They spend most of their time walking the leaves and watching for danger. When trouble comes, they are ready to give everything.

SUPER COLONIES

Swish! Argentine ants march in a line that stretches for miles.

Argentine ants originally come from South America but now live all over the world.

These small brown ants form supercolonies. That means millions of nests work together as one giant group. One supercolony in Europe stretches over 3,700 miles!

Argentine ants push out the native ants wherever they go. This hurts the balance of nature. Scientists are working hard to stop their spread before more native ants disappear.

Argentine ants from different nests never fight each other — they act like one big family!

PHARAOH'S PLAGUE

DID YOU KNOW?

Pharaoh ants got their name because people once thought they were one of the plagues of ancient Egypt!

Scratch! Tiny pharaoh ants sneak through a crack in the wall.

Pharaoh ants are some of the tiniest ants you will ever see. They are only about two millimeters long — smaller than a grain of rice!

These golden brown ants love warm buildings. They live in hospitals, kitchens, and stores. They squeeze through tiny cracks to find food and water. Even the smallest gap is big enough for them.

Pharaoh ants are very hard to get rid of. If one nest is bothered, the ants split up and make new nests. One colony can quickly become ten!

DRIVER INVASION

DID YOU KNOW?
In Africa, some people use driver ant jaws as natural stitches — the ants bite the wound closed, then the body is snipped off!

Crackle! Millions of driver ants flood the forest like a brown river.

Driver ants live in the forests of Africa. They are also called safari ants. Like army ants, they do not stay in one place. They march in long columns looking for food.

Driver ants have huge jaws and a painful bite. They attack anything in their path! Even large animals like elephants run away when driver ants come near.

A driver ant colony can have over 20 million ants. The queen is the biggest ant in the world — she can lay millions of eggs each month. No other ant comes close to her size.

EARTH'S HELPERS

Thud! An ant pushes out a ball of dirt ten times its own weight.

Ants do big things for our planet. They dig tunnels that let air and water reach plant roots. This keeps the soil healthy and helps plants grow strong.

Ants also spread seeds. Some ants carry seeds to new spots, and those seeds grow into fresh plants. Other ants eat dead bugs and leaves, cleaning up the forest floor like tiny garbage trucks.

These tiny insects keep nature running smoothly. We need to protect their wild homes so they can keep doing their important work.

TINY TITANS

Some ants have been found
trapped in amber that is over
100 million years old!

Tap! A long line of ants crosses the trail on tiny feet.

Next time you see ants, stop and watch them. See how they carry heavy loads. Watch how they work as a team. Ants are truly amazing!

You can help by leaving wild corners in your yard. A pile of sticks or leaves gives them a place to live. Do not spray bug poison near their nests — they need safe homes too.

Ants have been on Earth for over 100 million years. They marched alongside the dinosaurs and survived whatever wiped them out. Let's all do our part to make sure these tiny titans are still here for a long time to come.

GLOSSARY

colony
A large group of ants that live and work together.

mandibles
Strong jaws that ants use to bite and carry things.

antennae
Two feelers on an ant's head used to smell and touch.

pheromones
Special scents ants make to send messages to each other.

thorax
The middle part of an ant's body where its legs attach.